COOPER FLAGG

NBA STAR

By Charlie Beattie

Book design by Jake Nordby
Cover design by Jake Nordby

Photographs ©: David Becker/AP Images, cover, 1; Jess Stiles/Sipa USA/AP Images, 4, 23; Patrick Smith/Getty Images Sport/Getty Images, 7; Lance King/Getty Images Sport/Getty Images, 8; Ben McCanna/Portland Press Herald/Getty Images, 10; John Jones/Icon Sportswire, 13; Ethan Miller/Getty Images Sport/Getty Images, 14, 20; Brian Spurlock/Icon Sportswire, 16; Grant Halverson/Getty Images Sport/Getty Images, 18; Red Line Editorial, 22

Press Box Books, an imprint of Press Room Editions.

Library of Congress Control Number: 2025942705

ISBN
979-8-89469-068-1 (library bound)
979-8-89469-077-3 (paperback)
979-8-89469-094-0 (epub)
979-8-89469-086-5 (hosted ebook)

Distributed by North Star Editions, Inc.
2297 Waters Drive
Mendota Heights, MN 55120
www.northstareditions.com

Printed in the United States of America
012026

ABOUT THE AUTHOR

Charlie Beattie is a writer, editor, and former sportscaster. Originally from Saint Paul, Minnesota, he now lives in Charleston, South Carolina, with his wife and son.

TABLE OF CONTENTS

2

1

FLAGG DOES IT ALL

Cooper Flagg and the Duke Blue Devils were locked in a tight game with the Arizona Wildcats. The teams were battling in the Sweet 16 of the 2025 NCAA Tournament. The final seconds of the first half ticked down. Duke led 45–42. Arizona held on to the ball. The Wildcats wanted to take one last shot before halftime.

With seven seconds left, Arizona guard Caleb Love launched a long three-pointer.

Cooper Flagg drives to the basket during the 2025 Sweet 16.

His shot came up short. The rebound bounced to Duke forward Mason Gillis. He quickly handed it to Flagg. The freshman forward raced up court. But time was running out.

Flagg had to pull up several feet behind the three-point line. He unleashed a long shot from the edge of the half-court logo. The ball dropped in just before the halftime buzzer sounded. Teammates high-fived Flagg. Duke fans roared from the stands.

Flagg continued to shine after halftime. Early in the second half, he dribbled through two defenders. Then he spotted teammate Sion James open in the corner. Flagg whipped a no-look pass to the guard. James knocked down a key three-point shot.

Less than a minute later, Flagg caught the ball on the right wing. He dribbled to the

Kon Knueppel (left) celebrates after Flagg's buzzer-beater before halftime.

Flagg records one of his three blocks against Arizona.

middle of the court. Two defenders closed in on him. Flagg lobbed the ball to the rim. Duke center Khaman Maluach caught the pass in midair. Then he slammed in the dunk.

Arizona kept the game close. The Blue Devils led 86–77 with 5:24 left. The Wildcats stormed toward the Duke basket on a fast break. Flagg didn't give up on the play. He hustled back on defense. Arizona's K. J. Lewis rose for a layup. Flagg got to the basket first, though. The Duke freshman swatted the shot into the stands.

STAT STUFFER

Cooper Flagg did a bit of everything against Arizona. He scored 30 points. He dished out seven assists. He also added six rebounds and three blocks. Flagg's performance showed off all his impressive skills.

Duke fans celebrated a 100–93 victory. The Blue Devils advanced to the Elite Eight. And they could thank their star freshman for the win.

MONTVERDE
32
ACADEMY
MADE HOOPS
MONTVERDE
11
ACADEMY
MADE HOOPS

2

MAINE MAN

Cooper Flagg was born on December 21, 2006. He grew up in Newport, Maine. Both of Cooper's parents played college basketball. His mom, Kelly, coached the girls' varsity team at nearby Nokomis High School. Cooper and his twin brother, Ace, spent most of their free time practicing at the gym.

Cooper later starred at Nokomis. In 2022, he led the team to the state

Cooper (left) and Ace (right) played together throughout high school.

championship game as a freshman. Cooper scored 22 points and grabbed 16 rebounds. Nokomis won 43–27. Cooper was named Maine's Player of the Year after the season. He became the first freshman to ever win the award.

Cooper left Maine after his freshman season. He moved to Florida to attend Montverde Academy. The Flaggs thought the elite basketball school would give Cooper better training. Cooper also wanted to speed up his high school experience. He took extra classes to graduate a year early. That way, he could enter college in 2024.

At his new school, Cooper thrived on the court. He became the top recruit in the nation. College coaches loved his 6-foot-9 (206-cm) frame and versatile play. They also

Montverde Academy lost only three games during Cooper's two years there.

Cooper plays for the US select team in July 2024.

praised his winning attitude. Many of the country's top basketball colleges recruited Cooper. In October 2023, he committed to Duke University.

Cooper still had one more year at Montverde before he went to Duke. He led the team to an undefeated regular season. In March, the Eagles played in the high school national championship game. They faced a team from Virginia. Cooper wouldn't let his team lose. He scored 16 points in the final. Cooper added eight rebounds and six blocks. Montverde won 79–63.

RARE SELECTION

In June 2024, Team USA invited Cooper Flagg to a training camp. He played for the US select team with young players from the National Basketball Association (NBA). Flagg became the first amateur player invited to the camp in more than a decade. He nearly led his team to an upset win over the US men's Olympic team. The select team lost 74–73.

SPALDING
DUKE
2
EDWARDS JR.
5
Kroger
PNC

3

FLAGG FLIES HIGH

Cooper Flagg arrived at Duke with big expectations. In his first game, the Blue Devils hosted the Maine Black Bears. Cooper scored 18 points. He also recorded seven rebounds, five assists, and three steals. Duke won 96–62.

Flagg didn't slow down. He showed off all the skills that made him the nation's top recruit. In January 2025, the forward scored 42 points against Notre Dame in

Flagg averaged 1.4 blocks per game in 2024–25.

Flagg soars for a dunk during a 2025 game against Pittsburgh.

an Atlantic Coast Conference (ACC) game. Flagg set the conference record for points by a freshman.

Duke coach Jon Scheyer knew his star player could score like that every game. But Flagg preferred to play unselfish basketball.

He took pride in passing and getting his teammates involved. And on defense, Flagg could guard anyone on the floor. The freshman lifted Duke to the ACC title.

Flagg suffered an injury during the ACC Tournament. Fans worried he wouldn't be able to play in the NCAA Tournament. But he recovered in time.

The injury didn't bother Flagg at all. He continued to play well in the NCAA Tournament. After dominating against Arizona in the Sweet 16, Flagg helped Duke easily beat Alabama in the Elite Eight. The Blue Devils then faced Houston in the Final Four.

FINDING BALANCE

In college, Flagg earned many endorsement deals. In 2024, he signed a shoe deal with New Balance. The company wasn't as famous for basketball shoes as some other brands. But New Balance makes many of its shoes in Maine. Flagg liked having a home-state connection to the brand.

Flagg dunks during a 2025 NBA Summer League game.

Flagg played at his best on the big stage. He led his team in points, rebounds, assists, steals, and blocks against Houston. No player had ever done that in a Final Four game. But his performance wasn't enough. Houston won 70–67.

The Wooden and Naismith Awards each honor the best men's college basketball player in the country. Flagg won both awards for the 2024–25 season. He had nothing left to prove in college. After his freshman year, he declared for the NBA Draft. The Dallas Mavericks had the first overall pick. They used it on Flagg.

Flagg lived up to the hype of being the top recruit in high school. He had no problem dominating in college, either. Mavericks fans now hoped he'd be able to do the same in the NBA.

TIMELINE MAP

1. Newport, Maine: 2006
Cooper Flagg is born on December 21.

2. Portland, Maine: 2022
Flagg scores 22 points and adds 16 rebounds to lead his high school team to the Maine Class A state championship.

3. Montverde, Florida: 2022
Flagg transfers to Montverde Academy.

4. Brownsburg, Indiana: 2024
Flagg leads Montverde to the high school national championship.

5. Durham, North Carolina: 2025
Flagg sets an ACC freshman record by scoring 42 points for Duke against Notre Dame.

6. Newark, New Jersey: 2025
Behind Flagg's 30 points, Duke beats Arizona 100–93 in the Sweet 16.

7. San Antonio, Texas: 2025
Flagg becomes the first player to lead his team in points, rebounds, assists, steals, and blocks in a Final Four game.

8. Brooklyn, New York: 2025
The Dallas Mavericks select Flagg with the top pick in the NBA Draft.

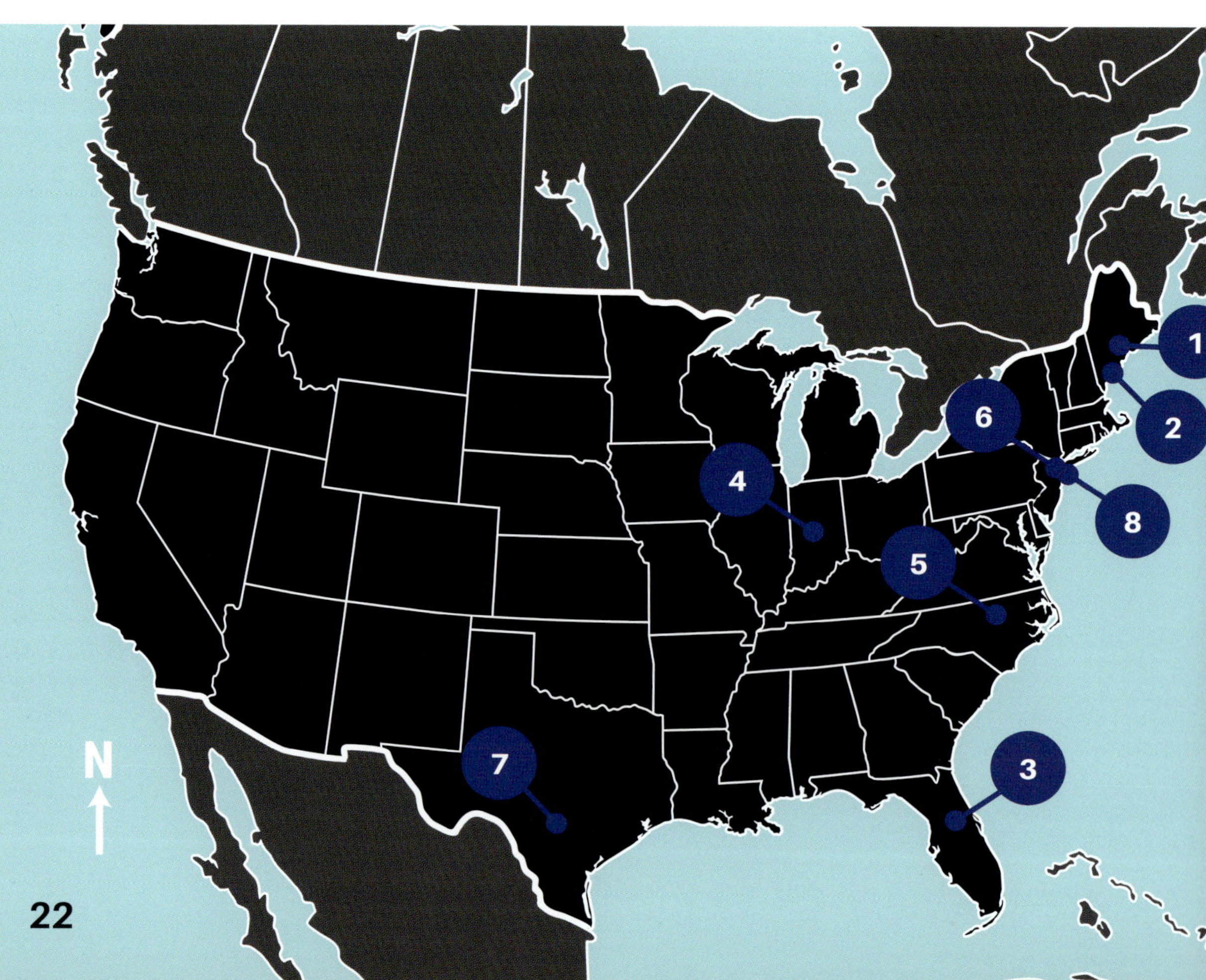

AT A GLANCE

COOPER FLAGG

Birth date: December 21, 2006

Birthplace: Newport, Maine

Position: Forward

Height: 6-foot-9 (206-cm)

Weight: 225 pounds (102 kg)

Current team: Dallas Mavericks (2025–)

Past team: Duke Blue Devils (2024–25)

Major awards: National Boys Basketball Player of the Year (2024), All-America First Team (2025), Wooden Award (2025), Naismith Award (2025)

Accurate through the 2024–25 season.

MORE INFORMATION

To learn more about Cooper Flagg, go to **pressboxbooks.com/AllAccess**.

These links are routinely monitored and updated to provide the most current information available.

GLOSSARY

amateur

Having to do with players who are not paid.

assists

Passes that lead directly to a teammate scoring a basket.

draft

An event that allows teams to choose new players coming into the league.

elite

The best of the best.

endorsement

When a person gets paid to speak in favor of a product or service.

freshman

A first-year student.

recruit

An athlete who college teams are interested in.

versatile

Able to perform many tasks well.

INDEX